Table of Contents

Bunny Hop,
page 6

Sassy Slide, **page 18**

Combat Boots,
page 21

Annie's® *Sew Slippers for Kids* is published by Annie's, 306 East Parr Road, Berne, IN 46711. Printed in USA. Copyright © 2012, 2014 Annie's. All rights reserved. This publication may not be reproduced in part or in whole without written permission from the publisher.

RETAIL STORES: If you would like to carry this pattern book or any other Annie's publications, visit AnniesWSL.com.

Every effort has been made to ensure that the instructions in this pattern book are complete and accur   human error, typographical mistakes or variations in individual work. Please visit AnniesCustomerCare.com to

ISBN: 978-1-59635-600-9

4 5 6 7 8 9 10 11

D1295630

Sew Slippers for Kids

For kids, the magical time between bath and bed time is the small part of the day when their fantasies are woven with fairy tales of princesses, explorers or trips to the moon. It is the time when dreams come true, awake becomes asleep, and the stars and moon dance overhead to the soft slumber of a small child.

In *Sew Slippers for Kids*, I've created an opportunity for you to indulge in your child's fantasy by stitching the magical slipper designs found between the pages of this book. Simple to stitch and fun to wear, I hope the designs inspire you to create you and your child's, or grandchild's, fantasy world. Whether you sew Smokin' Hot Wheels, Bunny Hop, Playful Puppies, Moroccan or one of the other designs, your child will believe that these slippers are the stuff that dreams are made of.

Enjoy creating these lovely slippers! ■

Meet the Designer

As a child, Julie Johnson was fascinated by her mother kneeling on the floor, smoothing the fabric and carefully pinning the pattern pieces. She loved to follow behind her, unpinning the patterns and placing the pins back into the cushion.

Julie began sewing at an early age, creating clothes for her Barbie® doll. She used a hand needle and thread, and scraps from her mother's dresses. She progressed to baby doll clothes, followed by the Catholic School white uniform blouses.

After receiving a clothing and textile degree from Madison Area Technical College, Julie was hired by two different sewing machine companies, and traveled around the country working at trade shows and state fairs, educating sewing machine dealers and consumers.

Currently, as a controller for five regional real estate offices with over 150 agents in upper Indiana, she still likes to sew, knit and crochet for relaxation after a busy day of crunching numbers. Her fascination with fiber and fabric has continued to evolve through the years. ■

General Instructions

Basic Sewing Supplies & Equipment

Besides a clean and fit sewing machine with a new needle in the appropriate size for your fabric and project, you will also need:

• Hand-sewing needles and thimble
• Marking pens
• Pattern tracing paper or cloth
• Pressing equipment
• Scissors
• Serger (optional)
• Straight pins and pincushion
• Seam ripper

Selecting the Right Size

The slipper patterns in this book have been designed with Extra-Small, Small, Medium and Large size choices. To determine which size to make, trace the sole patterns for each size onto paper or poster board and cut out.

Have the child step onto the pattern and use the size that comes closest to his/her foot size. Or, lay the patterns on a pair of the child's shoes. You can also measure the foot length, from big toe tip to back of heel, and width, across the widest area of the foot, and compare to the pattern sizes provided.

Fabric Selection

When selecting fabrics for your slippers, consider the following:

Choose tightly woven fat quarters for your designs. They may cost a bit more, but a higher thread count will increase the durability and life of the slipper.

Choose knits with a limited amount of stretch. They are easier to sew. Also, knit edges will not fray so there is no need to edge-finish.

Prewash your fashion fabric and anti-skid gripper fabric to remove the sizing. The sizing helps the manufacturer "weave" the fabric and creates a stiff hand that is not needed for sewing. With the sizing removed, the fabrics will shrink at the same rate, eliminating puckering.

Stabilize your fabric with a tricot-backed fusible interfacing. The interfacing will help prevent your cotton's woven edges from fraying and will increase the durability of the slipper.

Use mercerized cotton thread for stitching to increase durability.

Edge-finish woven fabrics with a small zigzag stitch with the "zag" slightly over the edge of the fabric or with a serged three- or four-thread stitch.

Avoid non-washable fabrics if laundering is desired. Look for the manufacturer's stamp on the fabric bolt or fat quarters to determine if the fabric can be laundered and how. You may also want to test a swatch of fabric to determine washability prior to stitching.

Stitching Specialty Fabrics

Specialty fabrics, like faux fur, can make cute and whimsical slippers. Just take a look at our Bunny Hop slippers on page 6. Knits are comfortable and easy-care choices. And applying an anti-skid gripper fabric, like Slipper Gripper sold through the Clotilde catalog, to the soles of your slippers makes them virtually slip-free.

Use the following tips to make sewing with these fabric choices easy.

Faux Fur

Position each pattern piece on the wrong side of the fabric and trace around pattern.

Use small scissors to make short clips on the fabric, keeping the point of the scissors close to the fabric. Go slowly so you clip as little of the fur as possible.

Use a ballpoint needle to avoid puncturing the knit stitches of the fabric (see Knits).

The fur can be slippery. Use additional pins as necessary to hold pieces together.

After stitching each seam, take the time to pull the fur from the seam. Run your fingers over the seam to loosen the fur from the seam. Use the blunt end of a seam ripper or a toothpick to pick fur from seam.

Avoid ironing the fur. It may melt. If pressing is needed, use a cool iron and press on the wrong side of the fabric.

Knits

Stabilize knit fabrics by fusing a lightweight knit interfacing to the back of the fabric. Be sure the stretch of the interfacing matches the stretch of the fabric. The interfacing will remove some of the "stretch" from the fabric, making it easier to sew, but will still stretch with the knit to give the slipper pucker-free seams.

Switch to a ballpoint needle. This has a rounded point that will slide between the knit's stitches, avoiding puncturing and creating runs in the fabric.

Stitch a sample seam on scraps. If your knit grows as you stitch, the pressure on your presser foot is adjusted too tight. Refer to your owner's manual on how to adjust it. Just remember to set it back when you are done stitching knits. Or, try a walking foot, which will help the fabric feed more evenly under the presser foot.

Anti-Skid Gripper Fabric

Anti-skid gripper fabric boasts rubber dots that are applied to one side of a light- to medium-weight canvas to make a fabric that will grip any surface while walking, running and jumping! It is a must for little ones with active feet.

Cut and baste a set of soles from the gripper fabric to slipper fabric soles. Keep the gripper rubber dots on the outside bottom of the soles.

Sewing can be a challenge because the rubber dots will keep your project from feeding through the sewing machine. To sew, cover the gripper fabric with tissue paper first, then it will glide evenly over your feed dogs and through your machine.

If you have problems with your needle breaking, try a heavy-duty needle, size 14 or 16. This will stitch through the denser rubber dots of the gripper fabric without breaking.

If you can't find a gripper fabric, you can substitute rubber, nonslip shelf liner. Use the same sewing techniques listed here.

Batting Selection

The designs in this book were stitched with 100 percent cotton, low-loft batting. The batting is stitched into the seam allowances to prevent shifting during laundering.

Or, use a fusible batting, which adheres to the body fabric, eliminates basting and prevents shifting when washing.

Polyester batting is thicker and will keep the slippers warmer. It is also machine washable and holds its shape better than cotton batting.

Bias binding

Many of the designs in this book use bias binding to cover the raw edges. Premade bias tape is available in a wide variety of colors and can be used; however, it is easy to make your own from coordinating fabrics that will really complement the design. Follow these simple steps:

1. Fold fabric diagonally so the crosswise grain straight edge is parallel to the selvage or lengthwise grain. Cut fabric along this fold line to mark the true bias (Figure 1).

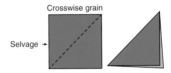

Figure 1

2. Using a clear ruler, mark successive bias lines the instructed width apart. Carefully cut along lines. Handle edges carefully to avoid stretching (Figure 2).

Figure 2

3. Sew short ends of strips together diagonally; press seams open making one long bias strip (Figure 3).

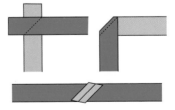

Figure 3

4. Fold and press bias strips as instructed in pattern to make bias binding for slippers.

Paper-Backed Fusible Web

Some projects in the book use a fusible web appliqué method to embellish the slippers. You can purchase fusible web in sheets or by the yard from several manufacturers. Follow the manufacturer's directions included with the brand purchased. Always finish the edges of fused shapes with hand- or machine-stitched blanket, zigzag or satin stitches to secure the shapes.

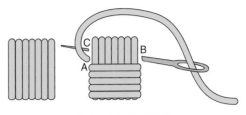

Padded Satin Stitch

Safety First

Some of the embellishments suggested in the patterns may not be suitable for children where choking may be a hazard. Snap-on eyes and noses can be replaced with embroidered satin or padded satin-stitched eyes and noses. Decorative buttons can be replaced with embroidered circles, purchased iron-on felt buttons or fusible appliquéd fabric circles. Any trims should be securely sewn to the slippers. ■

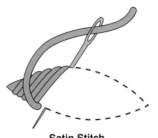

Satin Stitch

Bunny Hop

Hop your way to sleepy time with this adorable child's slipper stitched from fake fur and simple accent fabric and notions.

Materials

- Scraps dark pink cotton fabric
- ¼ yard white fake fur
- 4 snap-on black doll eyes
- 2 (½-inch) round black buttons
- 1 skein white medium-weight, worsted acrylic yarn
- 1 package anti-skid gripper fabric
- Basic sewing supplies and equipment

Cutting

Use pattern templates B1–B4 and S in size desired (pages 28–34). Transfer all pattern markings to fabric.

From white fake fur:
- Cut four Bunny Hop (B1) for body, reverse two.
- Cut four Bunny Hop Face (B2).
- Cut four Bunny Hop (B4) for body lining, reverse two.
- Cut two Bunny Hop Ears (B3).
- Cut two Soles (S) for lining; reverse one.

From dark pink cotton fabric:
- Cut two Bunny Hop Ears for lining (B3).

From anti-skid gripper fabric:
- Cut two Soles (S); reverse one.

Assembly

Instructions are given to stitch one slipper; repeat to make second slipper. Stitch right sides together using a ¼-inch seam allowance unless otherwise indicated. Refer to Fake Fur Tips on page 3 for helpful hints.

1. To make slipper upper, stitch fake fur and dark pink ears together leaving bottom open. Turn ears right side out.

2. Fold outside edge of ear to ¼ inch from opposite edge and pin to hold. Reverse to make second ear (Figure 1).

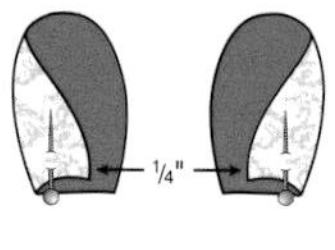

Figure 1

3. Stitch heel and center front seams of B1 and toe seam of B2 for body (Figure 2).

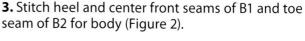

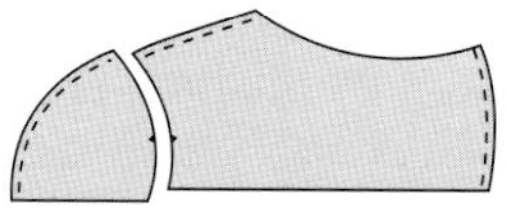

Figure 2

4. Position unfolded edge of ears on either side of B1 front seam; pin and baste to hold (Figure 3).

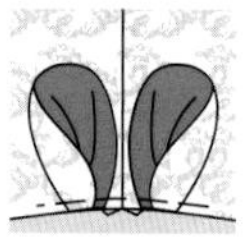

Figure 3

5. Stitch B1 and B2 together matching notches and completing slipper upper.

6. To add sole to slipper upper, pin and stitch anti-skid gripper fabric sole to slipper upper matching heel seam to sole center back and center front seam to sole center front at toe. Trim and clip seam. Set aside.

7. To make slipper lining, stitch B4 lining heel and center front seam, leaving open for turning between A and B (Figure 4).

Figure 4

8. Stitch fake fur Sole to slipper lining referring to step 5. Turn right side out.

9. Slip lining inside slipper, right sides together. Pin lining top edge to slipper top edge and stitch.

10. Turn slipper and lining right side out through lining opening.

11. Make a small hole in slipper fabric at eye placement and insert eye. Reach to wrong side of fabric through lining opening and snap eye backing into

place. Stitch button nose at placement marking through slipper upper only.

12. Turn lining seam allowances to inside and hand- or machine-stitch closed. Slip lining inside slipper.

13. To make a pompom for bunny tail, cut 6-inch piece of yarn from skein. Cut a 4-inch square of cardboard. Wrap yarn from skein around cardboard at least 30 times.

14. Slide yarn off cardboard and wrap tightly around middle with 6-inch piece of yarn, tying off to secure.

15. Cut yarn loops at both ends and fluff to make pompom. Trim as needed.

16. Hand-stitch pompom about 1 inch from top of slipper at center back. ■

Flower Power

Easy to stitch and fun to wear—create a warm and colorful slipper accented with a colorful flower.

Materials
- 1 coordinating fat quarter
- ¼ yard polar fleece
- ⅛ yard quilt batting
- 1 package anti-skid gripper fabric
- Basic sewing supplies and equipment

Cutting
Use pattern templates F and S in size desired (pages 28–31, 35). Transfer all pattern markings to fabric.

From polar fleece:
- Cut four Flower Power Uppers (F), reverse two.
- Cut two Soles (S); reverse one.

From coordinating fat quarter:
- Cut four Flower Power Uppers (F), reverse two.

From quilt batting:
- Cut two Soles (S); reverse one.

From anti-skid gripper fabric:
- Cut two Soles (S); reverse one.

Assembly
Instructions are given to stitch one slipper; repeat to make second slipper. Stitch right sides together using a ¼-inch seam allowance unless otherwise indicated.

1. Stitch two coordinating fat quarter F uppers together at center back seam (Figure 1). Repeat with two fleece lining F uppers.

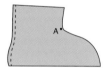

Figure 1

2. Stitch front seam from toe center front to A for both coordinating fat quarter and fleece lining (Figure 2). Using a tailor's ham, press seam allowances flat.

Figure 2

3. Baste batting S to wrong side of fleece lining S.

4. Pin and stitch anti-skid gripper fabric sole to coordinating fat quarter F, right sides together matching center back and front seams to sole center front and back (Figure 3). Trim and clip sole seams as needed.

Figure 3

Reverse outer and lining fabrics for a different look.

5. Repeat steps 1–4 using fleece lining F and S, leaving 3–4-inch opening along sole side. Turn right side out through opening.

6. Slip fleece lining F inside coordinating fat quarter F, right sides together. Pin top edges together and stitch. Turn right side out through the opening along sole side.

7. Turn lining seam allowances to inside and hand-stitch together with whipstitch (Figure 4). Slip lining inside slipper.

Figure 4

8. Press seam flat and topstitch around slipper top, pivoting at A to stitch across front seam.

9. Refer to Fabric Flower (page 10) to make flower embellishments. Position flowers on center front seam referring to photos. Wear with slipper top up or rolled down as desired. ■

Wear cuff up or down.

Fabric Flower

A bouquet of stitched flowers will brighten any girl's day. Stitch the flower onto a jewelry backing to make the bouquet attach to slippers quickly and easily.

Materials
- Scraps coordinating cotton
- Scraps coordinating felt
- Scraps paper-backed fusible web
- Accent buttons
- Metal jewelry clasp
- Seam sealant
- Basic sewing supplies and equipment

Assembly
1. Cut a 3 x 10½-inch rectangle from scrap cotton.

2. Fold strip in half lengthwise, right sides together, and gently press.

3. Stitch five half-moon shapes approximately 2 inches apart and ¼ inch away from rectangle raw edges to make flower petals (Figure 1). *Note: Curves are easy to draw when you use a round household item as a template, like a coffee cup.* Cut seam allowances around shapes to ⅛ inch.

Figure 1

4. Clip into "v" created between each flower petal. Apply a drop of seam sealant between petals at bottom of "v." Let dry.

5. Turn each petal right side out through bottom. Run finger along seam on inside to smooth seam. Press flat.

Change fabric and button styles to create different looks for your flower.

6. Finish bottom edge of petal strip with zigzag, overedge stitch or serger (Figure 2).

Figure 2

7. Hand-sew gathering stitches along the straight edge of the petal strip. Pull thread to gather, creating the center of the flower (Figure 3). Tie off thread tails and secure thread on the back of the flower.

Figure 3

8. Position and stitch button on flower center.

9. Trace a ¾-inch circle onto paper side of paper-backed fusible web scrap. Cut out, leaving margin around circle. Fuse circle to felt scrap and cut out on traced line.

10. Remove paper and hand-stitch non-fusible side of felt circle to jewelry clasp.

11. Position circle on the flower center back and carefully fuse into place using the point of your iron. **Note:** *Take a few stitches through felt and flower back for added security.*

12. Attach completed flower to slipper as desired. ■

Playful Puppies

These adorable puppy slippers will quickly become your child's best friend.

Materials

- ¼ yard brown fake fur
- ¼ yard coordinating cotton fabric
- ⅛ yard quilt batting
- 4 snap-on doll eyes
- 2 snap-on animal noses
- Small package polyester stuffing
- 1 package anti-skid gripper fabric
- Basic sewing supplies and equipment

Cutting

Use pattern templates P1–P5 and S in size desired (pages 28–31, 36–38). Transfer all pattern markings to fabric.

From brown fake fur:
- Cut four Playful Puppies Body (P1); reverse two.
- Cut four Playful Puppies Body Center (P2); reverse two.
- Cut four Playful Puppies Toe (P3); reverse two.
- Cut two Playful Puppies Ears (P4).

From coordinating cotton fabric:
- Cut two Playful Puppies Ears (P4).
- Cut four Playful Puppies Lining (P5); reverse two.
- Cut two Soles (S) for lining; reverse one.

From anti-skid gripper fabric:
- Cut two Soles (S); reverse one.

From quilt batting:
- Cut two Soles (S); reverse one.

Assembly

Instructions are given to stitch one slipper; repeat to make second slipper. Stitch right sides together using a ¼-inch seam allowance unless otherwise indicated. Refer to Fake Fur Tips on page 3 for helpful hints.

1. To make slipper upper, stitch brown fake fur and coordinating cotton fabric P4 ears together leaving open at bottom. Turn right side out and set aside.

2. Stitch center front and heel seams of two P1 body pieces.

3. Pin and stitch center front seam of two P2 body centers and curved center front seam of two P3 toes (Figure 1).

Figure 1

4. Position fake fur side of ears ¼ inch on either side of right side of P1 center front seam and baste (Figure 2).

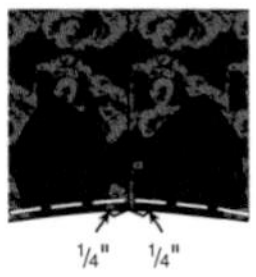

Figure 2

5. Stitch P2 and P3 together matching center front seams and double notches (Figure 3).

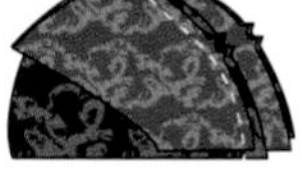

Figure 3

6. Stitch P1 and P2/P3 together matching center front seams and single notches.

7. To add sole to slipper upper, pin and stitch anti-skid gripper fabric sole to slipper upper matching heel seam to sole center back and center front seam to sole center front at toe. Trim and clip seam. Set aside.

8. To make slipper lining, pin and stitch P5 lining heel and center front seam leaving open between A and B for turning (Figure 4).

Figure 4

Sew Slippers for Kids

9. Layer lining and batting soles wrong sides together and baste. Stitch lining/batting sole to P5, lining right sides together, referring to step 7. Turn right side out.

10. Slip lining inside slipper, right sides together. Pin lining top edge to slipper top edge and stitch (Figure 5).

Figure 5

11. Turn slipper and lining right side out through lining opening.

12. Make a small hole in slipper fabric at eye placement and insert eye. Reach to wrong side of fabric through lining opening and snap eye backing into place. Repeat for nose.

13. Lightly stuff slipper toe with polyester fiberfill through lining opening to make a firm nose.

14. Turn lining seam allowances to inside and hand- or machine-stitch closed. Slip lining inside slipper.

15. Push lining under and around the stuffing at toe. Hand-stitch lining to slipper at seam below eyes to hold stuffing and lining in place.

16. Stitch lining to slipper upper along heel seams to hold lining in place.

17. Lightly brush seams with fingertips to pull fur from each seam. If necessary, use the point of small scissors or seam ripper to pull fur from seams, taking care to not pull fur from fabric. Repeat for fur behind eyes and nose. ∎

Sole Power

Pump up the power with a stuffed sole for your child's slipper.

Materials
- ¼ yard stretch velour
- 4 coordinating fat quarters (A, B, C and D)
- ⅛ yard quilt batting
- Clover Flower Frill Templates
- 12 x 12 x 2-inch square high density outdoor upholstery foam
- 1 package anti-skid gripper fabric
- Basic sewing supplies and equipment

Cutting
Use pattern templates SP1–SP3 and S in size desired (pages 28–31, 42–43). Transfer all pattern markings to fabric.

Set aside coordinating fat quarters B, C and D to make Flower Frills.

From stretch velour:
- Cut two Sole Power Toe Front (SP1).
- Cut two Sole Power Toe Lining (SP3).

- Cut two sole bands for desired size as listed below:
    18 x 1¼-inch Extra-Small
    19 ½ x 1¼-inch Small
    21 x 1¼-inch Medium
    22½ x 1¼-inch Large

- Cut two heel bands for desired size as listed below:
    6½ x 3-inch Extra-Small
    7 x 3-inch Small
    7½ x 3½-inch Medium
    8½ x 3½-inch Large

From coordinating fat quarter A:
- Cut two Sole Power Toe Tab (SP2).
- Cut two Soles (S); reverse one.

From quilt batting:
- Cut two Sole Power Toe Lining (SP3).
- Cut two heel bands for desired size as listed below:
    6½ x 1½-inch Extra-Small
    7 x 1½-inch Small
    7½ x 1¾-inch Medium
    8½ x 1¾-inch Large

- Cut two Soles (S); reverse one.

From high density outdoor upholstery foam:
Cut two Soles (S); reverse one. *Note: Trace Sole template onto foam. Draw cutting line about ⅛ inch inside template traced line. Cut on this cutting line with a serated knife.*

From anti-skid gripper fabric:
- Cut two Soles (S); reverse one.

Assembly

Instructions are given to stitch one slipper; repeat to make second slipper. Stitch right sides together using a ¼-inch seam allowance unless otherwise indicated.

1. Sew SP2 to SP1 along straight edge, press seam toward SP2. Topstitch seam to SP2 (Figure 1).

Figure 1

2. Position quilt batting heel band on wrong side of velour heel band. Fold heel band in half lengthwise over quilt batting and press. Topstitch along folded edge (Figure 2).

Figure 2

3. Position and stitch heel band to toe matching raw edges to toe straight edge with folded edge of heel band toward center of toe (Figure 3).

Figure 3

4. Layer toe, with heel band attached, right side up; SP3 lining, wrong side up and SP3 batting. Stitch through all layers across straight edge (Figure 4).

Figure 4

5. Flip batting and lining over seam and pull heel band away from seam. Press and topstitch seam referring again to Figure 4.

6. Baste batting sole to wrong side of coordinating fat quarter sole. Pin and stitch coordinating fat quarter side of sole to lining side of toe and heel band to complete the slipper upper (Figure 5). Set aside.

Figure 5

7. Stitch short ends of sole band together and press seam open. Pin and stitch sole band to anti-skid gripper fabric sole right sides together (Figure 6).

Figure 6

8. Pin raw edge of sole band to slipper upper right sides together. Stitch, leaving a 3–4-inch opening. Turn right side out through opening.

9. Insert high density foam sole into slipper through opening. Tuck opening edges to inside and hand-stitch opening closed.

10. Using the Clover Flower Frill templates and manufacturer's instructions, make a flower with coordinating fat quarters B, C and D. Refer to photo to center and position flower on tab and hand-stitch in place. ■

Sassy Slide

Create this slipper in about an hour, and turn your little girl's step into a sassy slide.

Materials
- Scraps coordinating green
- ¼ yard bright floral
- 1 fat quarter coordinating tonal or solid
- 2 (1½-inch) flower buttons
- 2 (1-inch) coordinating flower buttons
- 1 package anti-skid gripper fabric
- Basic sewing supplies and equipment

Cutting
Use pattern templates SS1, SS2 and S in size desired (pages 28–31, 39). Transfer all pattern markings to fabric.

From bright floral:
- Cut four Sassy Slide Toes (SS1).
- Cut two Soles (S); reverse one.

From coordinating tonal or solid:
- Cut total of 48 inches of 1¼-inch-wide bias strips for binding.

From scraps coordinating green:
- Cut eight Sassy Slide Leaves (SS2).

From quilt batting:
- Cut two Sassy Slide Toes (SS1).
- Cut two Soles (S); reverse one.
- Cut four Sassy Slide Leaves (SS2).

From anti-skid gripper fabric:
- Cut two Soles (S); reverse one.

Assembly
Instructions are given to stitch one slipper; repeat to make second slipper. Stitch right sides together using a ¼-inch seam allowance unless otherwise indicated.

1. Layer anti-skid gripper fabric sole, wrong side up, batting and bright floral sole, right side up (Figure 1). Baste together and set aside.

Figure 1

2. Layer two bright floral SS1 right sides together onto a batting SS1. Stitch along top concave curve (Figure 2).

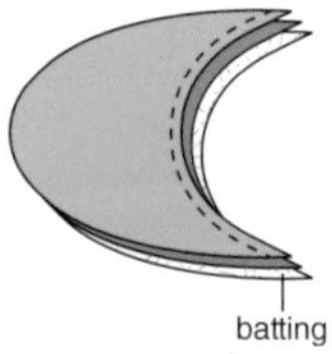

Figure 2

3. Press seam, trim and clip curve. Turn top bright floral layer to right side. Topstitch curved seam. Trim layers even to complete toe.

4. Pin and stitch completed SS1 to sole matching center fronts and toe raw edges.

5. To apply binding, press 1¼-inch strips in half lengthwise wrong sides together. Open, and press one long raw edge to center.

6. Fold binding short end ¼ inch to wrong side. Begin with folded short end on slipper center side and pin binding to anti-skid gripper fabric side of sole matching raw edges and overlapping ends. Stitch into place with ¼-inch seam (Figure 3).

Figure 3

7. Fold binding over raw edges of sole and toe to slipper top and pin. Edgestitch binding to complete slipper.

8. To make leaves for flower embellishment, layer one batting SS2 on top of two coordinating green SS2 leaves right sides together.

9. Stitch ⅛-inch seam allowance around curved edges, leaving bottom open. Turn right side out and press.

10. Topstitch a curved line through center of leaf from bottom to leaf point (Figure 4). Draw thread ends to back and secure in place by hand.

11. Fold a tuck in leaf bottom edge and stitch to hold.

12. Repeat steps 8–11 to make two leaves.

13. Refer to photos to position and hand-stitch leaves at top edge of toe.

14. Center, stack and hand-stitch small and large flower buttons on leaves. ■

Figure 4

Combat Boots

Give new life to old denim by transforming a pair
of cast-off jeans into a pair of Combat Boots.

Materials
- 1 pair child's size old jeans
- ¼ yard or coordinating fat quarter
- ¼ yard quilt batting
- 4 (⅝-inch) black buttons
- 1 package anti-skid gripper fabric
- Basic sewing supplies and equipment

Cutting
Use pattern templates C1 and S in size desired
(pages 28–31, 40). Transfer all pattern markings
to fabric.

From old jeans, for slipper:
- Remove back pockets and four belt loops,
  set aside.
- Cut four Combat Boots (C1), placing leg seam
  along placement line. Reverse two.

From coordinating fat quarter, for lining:
- Cut four Combat Boots (C1), reverse two.
- Cut two Sole (S) pieces, reverse one.

From quilt batting:
- Cut four Combat Boots (C1), reverse two.
- Cut two Sole (S) pieces, reverse one.

From anti-skid gripper fabric:
- Cut two Sole (S) pieces, reverse one.

Assembly
Instructions are given to stitch one slipper; repeat
to make second slipper. Stitch right sides together
using a ¼-inch seam allowance unless otherwise
indicated.

1. To make slipper upper, layer batting on wrong
side of denim C1 body. Sew body heel seam
together. Press seam open and lay flat with denim
side up.

2. Position and stitch pocket 1¼ inches from top,
and ¾ inch from front (Figure 1). **Note:** *Position
will vary with size of pocket. Reverse positioning for
second slipper.*

Figure 1

Tips & Techniques

*You can easily stitch these slippers from
recycled jeans, but if the pockets are too large
for your slippers, use the optional pocket
template C2 on page 41.*

- *Cut pocket from fabric the size desired to fit
  slipper size.*

- *Fold pocket right sides together along fold
  line and stitch, leaving 2–3 inches open on
  one side. Turn right side out through opening.*

- *Turn opening seam allowances to inside and
  press edges flat.*

- *Position pocket referring to step 2 of Combat
  Boots assembly instructions. Edgestitch
  along pocket sides and bottom.*

- *If desired, topstitch ⅛–¼ inch from first stitching.*

3. Position ends of one belt loop, right sides together on pocket side of slipper upper, ¼ inch from the top. Position second loop ⅜ inch from first loop and above A to make button loops (Figure 2). Baste in place.

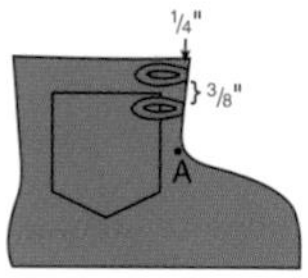

Figure 2

4. Stitch center front seam from toe to A on denim C1 (Figure 3). Using a tailor's ham, press seam allowances flat.

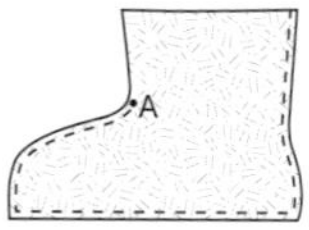

Figure 3

5. To add sole to slipper upper; match, layer and stitch anti-skid gripper fabric and batting S pieces wrong sides together.

6. Pin and stitch layered S pieces to denim C1, matching heel seam to S center back and front seam to S center front. Trim and clip seam.

7. To make lining, stitch lining C1 heel seam and lining C1 center front seam, leaving open between B and C for turning (Figure 4).

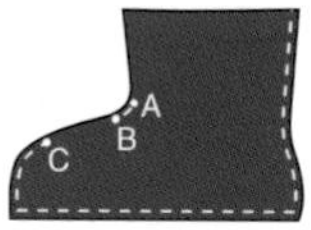

Figure 4

8. Repeat step 4 with C1 and S lining pieces, matching C1 seams to S centers. Turn right side out.

9. Slip lining inside slipper, right sides together, and pin lining to slipper matching A and center back seams. Stitch.

10. Clip corners by trimming corner flat, then trimming seam to corner (Figure 5).

Figure 5

11. Turn slipper and lining right side out through lining opening. Press seam allowances to inside and hand- or machine-stitch closed. Slip lining inside slipper.

12. Press seam flat and top stitch around slipper top pivoting at A to stitch across front seam (Figure 6).

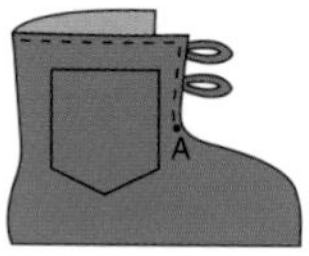

Figure 6

13. Press button loops into a point and stitch across point to secure. Push button loop flat against opposite side of slipper, mark and stitch black buttons in place. ■

Smokin' Hot Wheels

Rev up any little boy's engine by stitching him some smokin' hot wheels.

Materials
- Scraps coordinating cotton
- ⅛ yard black
- ¼ yard each two coordinating cottons (A, B)
- ⅛ yard quilt batting
- 8 (¾-inch) coordinating buttons
- Scraps paper-backed fusible web
- 1 package anti-skid gripper fabric
- Basic sewing supplies and equipment

Cutting
Use pattern templates H1–H4 and S in size desired (pages 28–31, 45–46). Transfer all pattern markings to fabric.

From cotton A:
- Cut four Hot Wheels Body (H1) for slipper upper; reverse two.

From cotton B:
- Cut four Hot Wheels Body (H1) for lining; reverse two.
- Cut two Soles (S) for lining; reverse one.

From black:
- Cut two 1¼-inch by fabric width strips for binding.
- Set aside remnants for wheels.

From quilt batting:
- Cut four Hot Wheels Body (H1); reverse two.
- Cut two Soles (S); reverse one.

From anti-skid gripper fabric:
- Cut two Soles (S); reverse one.

Assembly

Instructions are given to stitch one slipper; repeat to make second slipper. Stitch right sides together using a ¼-inch seam allowance unless otherwise indicated.

1. Trace two each H3 and H4 hubcaps and H2 front and back wheels onto paper side of paper-backed fusible web ¼ inch apart. Cut out, leaving ⅛-inch margin around each piece.

2. Fuse the H2 front and back wheels to wrong side of black remnants and H3 and H4 to wrong side of scraps. Cut out on traced lines.

3. Remove paper backing from hubcaps. Fuse hubcaps to wheels referring to Figure 1 and the placement drawing on page 46.

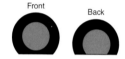

Figure 1

4. Remove paper backing from wheel unit. Fuse wheel unit to right and left H1 bodies as marked on templates (Figure 2). Edgestitch around the hubcaps and the wheels.

Figure 2

5. Baste batting sole to wrong side of sole lining. Set aside.

6. Pin right and left H1 bodies together at heel and stitch. Repeat with H1 lining and batting.

7. Press H1 body and lining seams open, clipping as needed. Trim batting seam to ⅛ inch.

8. Layer H1 lining, wrong side up; H1 batting and H1 body, right side up, matching heel seams and raw edges. Baste together and trim edges even if necessary (Figure 3).

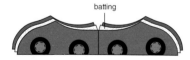

Figure 3

9. Press 1¼-inch strips in half lengthwise wrong sides together. Open and press one long raw edge to center.

10. Pin binding raw edge right side to lining side of layered slipper upper top edge and stitch.

11. Fold binding to H1 body side over raw edges and stitch.

12. Pin and stitch slipper body, lining sides together, along center front from toe to square matching bound curved edges (Figure 4). Press and pin seam open at toe.

Figure 4

13. Pin anti-skid gripper fabric Sole S right side to H1 body side of slipper upper matching raw edges, center front and back seams to sole center front and back. Keep slipper upper out of seam area and stitch (Figure 5).

Figure 5

14. Fold slipper upper to center of anti-skid gripper fabric right side. Pin right side of lining sole to right side of slipper lining matching raw edges to anti-skid gripper fabric edges. Stitch together leaving 3–4 inches open (Figure 6).

Figure 6

15. Turn slipper right side out through opening. Turn opening seam allowances to inside and whipstitch closed by hand. Sew ¾-inch buttons to centers of wheel appliqués to finish. ∎

Tips & Techniques

To create a version for your little girl, choose cotton fabric with a floral or butterfly design. Fuse paper-backed fusible web to wrong side of fabric scraps following manufacturer's instructions. Fussy-cut motifs from scraps, remove paper and fuse to slipper body in a pleasing pattern.

Moroccan

Find the princess in your little girl by stitching these colorful, fanciful slippers in brocade accented with a stash of jewels.

Materials
- ⅓ yard washable satin brocade
- 1 fat quarter coordinating cotton
- ⅓ yard quilt batting
- 10 (1 x ¾-inch) oval sew-on jewels
- 14 (1-inch) sew-on gold coin sequins
- 12 x 12-inch paper-backed fusible web
- 1 package anti-skid gripper fabric
- Basic sewing supplies and equipment

Cutting
Use pattern templates M and S in size desired (pages 28–31, 44). Transfer all pattern markings to fabric.

From washable satin brocade:
- Cut two Moroccan Toes (M).
- Cut one 12-inch square.

From coordinating cotton:
- Cut total of 90 inches of 1¼-inch bias strips for binding.

From quilt batting:
- Cut one Moroccan Toe (M), cut in half on fold line.
- Cut two 12-inch squares.

From anti-skid gripper fabric:
- Cut one 12-inch square.

Assembly
Instructions are given to stitch one slipper; repeat to make second slipper. Stitch right sides together using a ¼-inch seam allowance unless otherwise indicated.

1. To make both slipper soles, fuse paper-backed fusible web square to wrong side of satin 12-inch square following manufacturer's instructions. Remove paper and fuse satin to batting square.

2. Trace two Soles (S), reversing one, onto satin side of square and stitch on marked line.

3. Layer anti-skid gripper fabric square, wrong side up; second batting square and stitched satin/batting square, satin side up. Baste through all layers ¼ inch inside first stitching (Figure 1). Cut out around first stitching. Set aside.

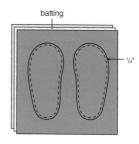

Figure 1

4. To make slipper upper, position and pin batting M to wrong side of satin M matching curved edges (Figure 2).

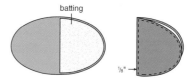

Figure 2

5. Fold satin M on fold line and over batting matching curved edges. Staystitch through all layers ⅛ inch from curved edges referring again to Figure 2. Trim batting even with satin if necessary and clip curves.

6. Position and pin slipper upper on sole matching center fronts and curved raw edges; baste (Figure 3).

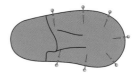

Figure 3

7. Cut a 2-inch piece from binding strip. Press raw edges to strip center. Then press in half. Stitch along both long sides to make back loop.

8. Position and pin back loop ends on either side of center back on satin side of sole, matching raw edges (Figure 4).

Figure 4

9. To apply binding, press 1¼-inch strips in half lengthwise wrong sides together. Open, and press one long raw edge to center.

10. Fold binding short end ¼ inch to wrong side. Begin with folded short end on slipper side center and pin binding to anti-skid gripper fabric side of sole matching raw edges and overlapping ends. Stitch into place with ¼-inch seam (Figure 5).

Figure 5

11. Fold binding over raw edges of sole and toe to slipper top and pin. Edgestitch binding to complete slipper.

12. Refer to photo and hand-stitch gold coin sequins and jewels as desired. ■

Pattern Templates

Cutting Lines

Extra-Small ————
Small ————
Medium ————
Large ————

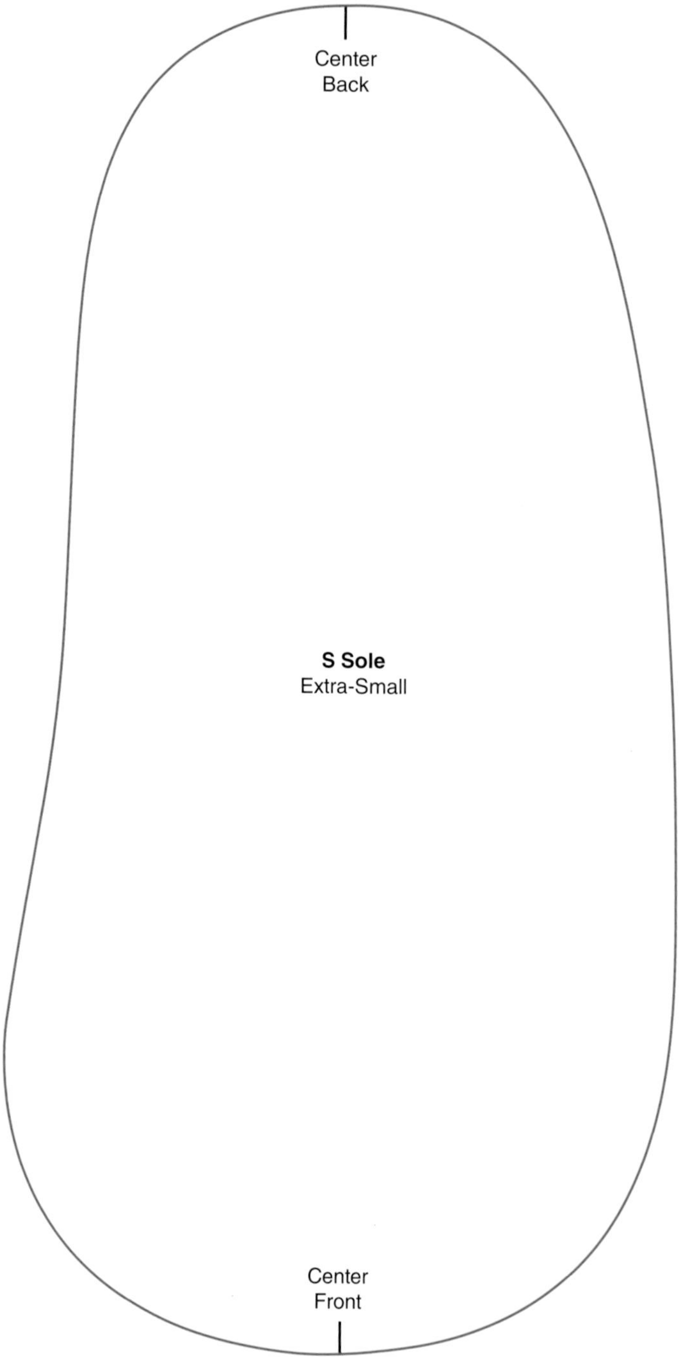

Center
Back

S Sole
Extra-Small

Center
Front

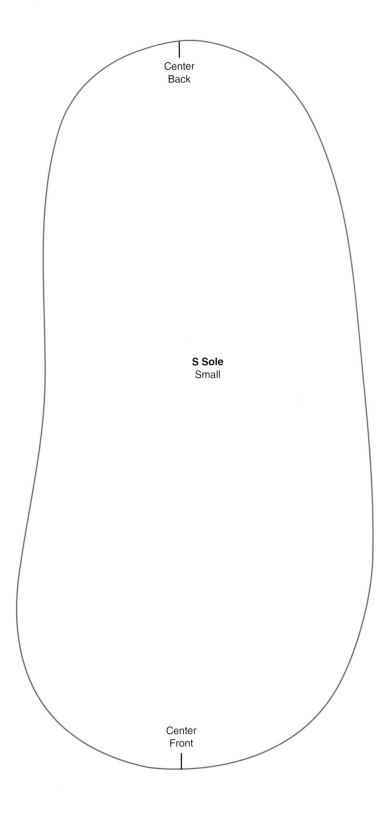

Center
Back

S Sole
Small

Center
Front

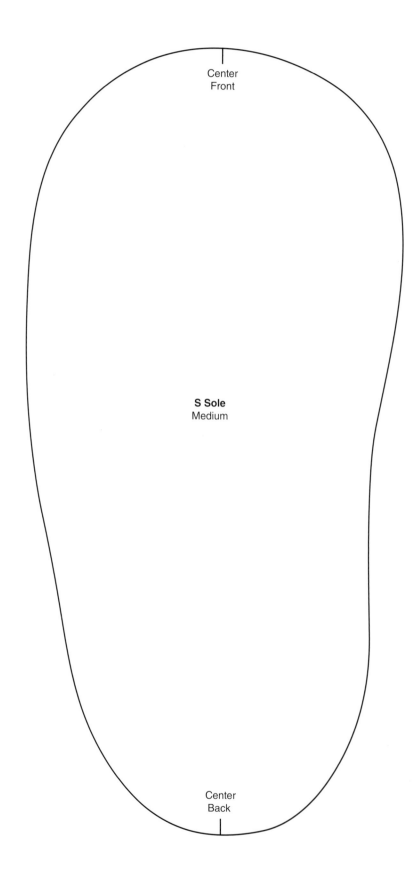

Center
Front

S Sole
Medium

Center
Back

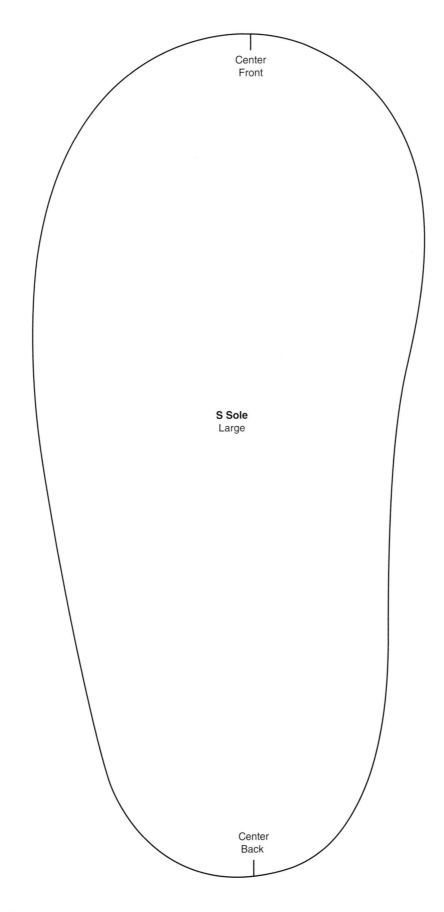

Center
Front

S Sole
Large

Center
Back

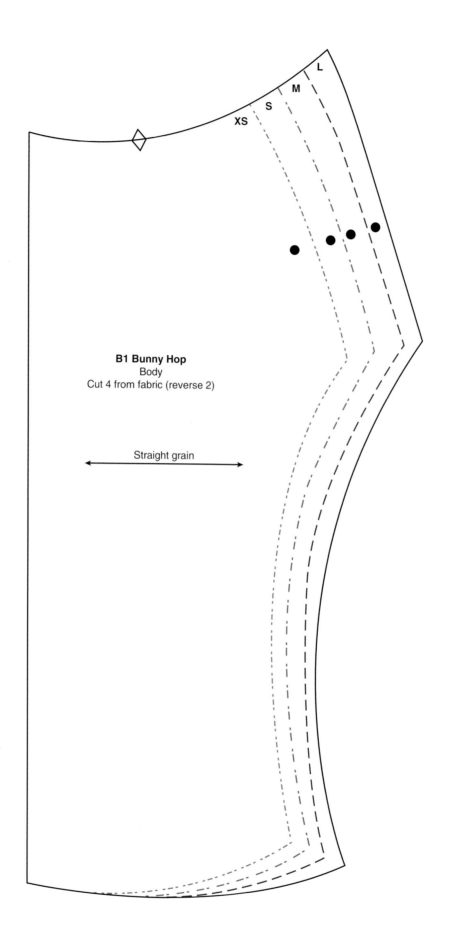

B1 Bunny Hop
Body
Cut 4 from fabric (reverse 2)

Straight grain

XS

S

M

L

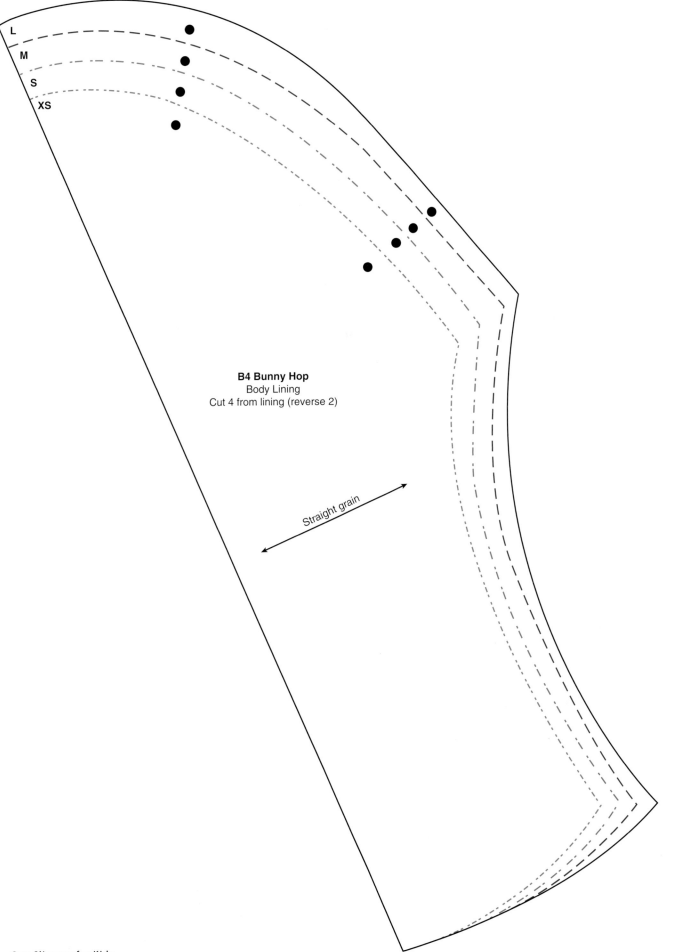

L

M

S

XS

B4 Bunny Hop
Body Lining
Cut 4 from lining (reverse 2)

Straight grain

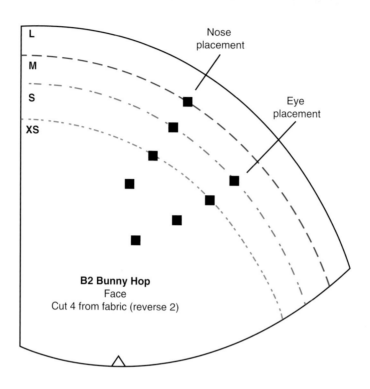

L

M

S

XS

Nose placement

Eye placement

B2 Bunny Hop
Face
Cut 4 from fabric (reverse 2)

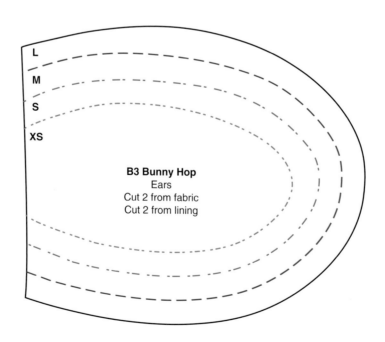

L

M

S

XS

B3 Bunny Hop
Ears
Cut 2 from fabric
Cut 2 from lining

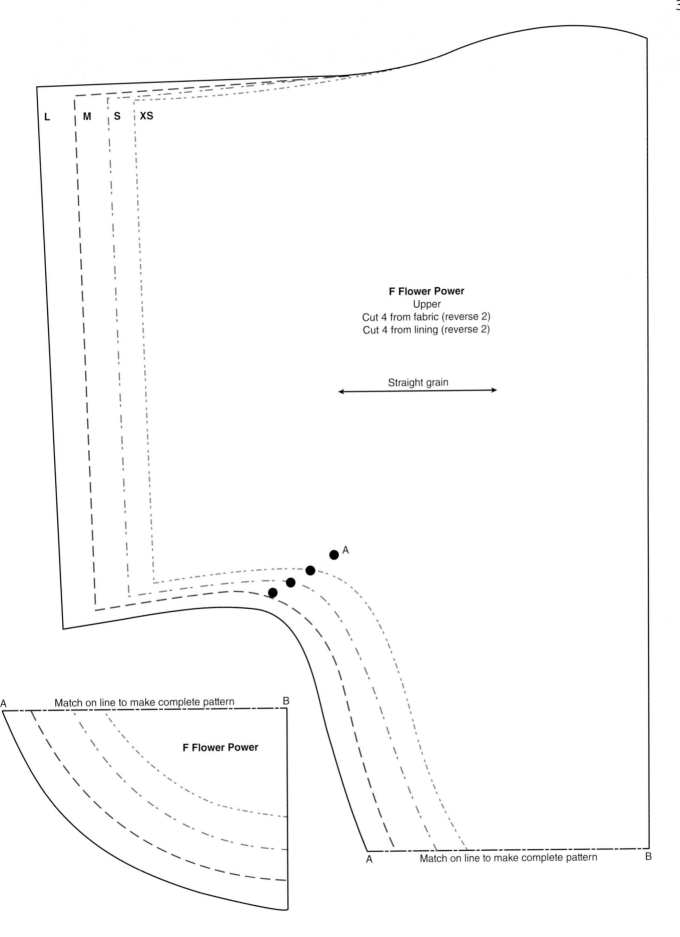

L M S XS

F Flower Power
Upper
Cut 4 from fabric (reverse 2)
Cut 4 from lining (reverse 2)

Straight grain

A

A   Match on line to make complete pattern   B

F Flower Power

A   Match on line to make complete pattern   B

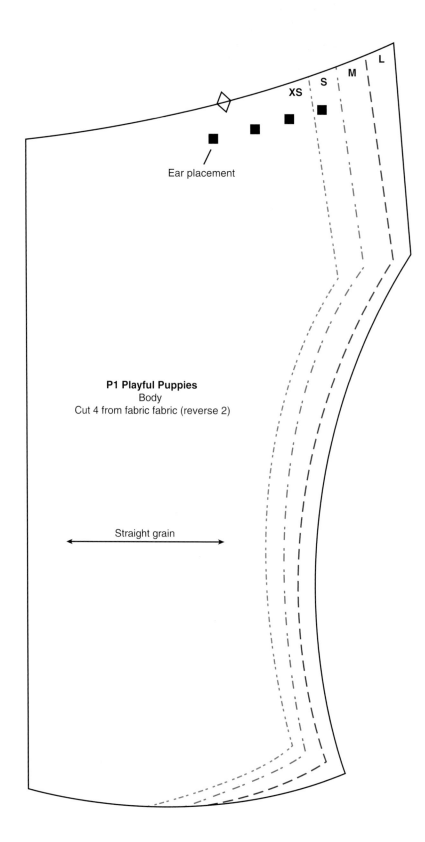

Ear placement

XS S M L

P1 Playful Puppies
Body
Cut 4 from fabric fabric (reverse 2)

Straight grain

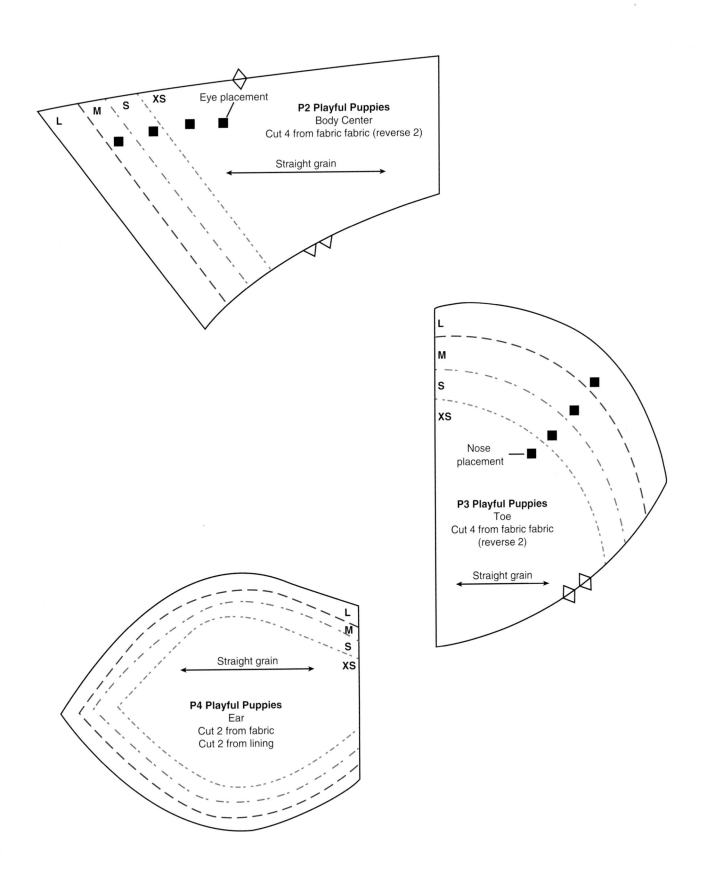

Eye placement

P2 Playful Puppies
Body Center
Cut 4 from fabric fabric (reverse 2)

Straight grain

L M S XS

L

M

S

XS

Nose
placement

P3 Playful Puppies
Toe
Cut 4 from fabric fabric
(reverse 2)

Straight grain

Straight grain

L
M
S
XS

P4 Playful Puppies
Ear
Cut 2 from fabric
Cut 2 from lining

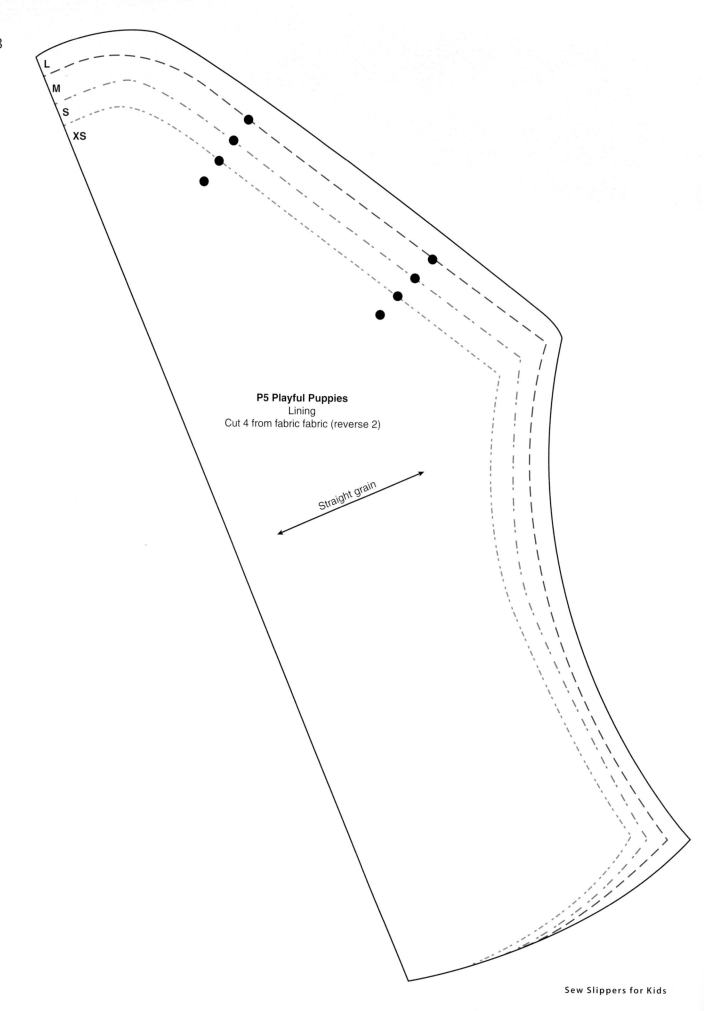

L
M
S
XS

P5 Playful Puppies
Lining
Cut 4 from fabric fabric (reverse 2)

Straight grain

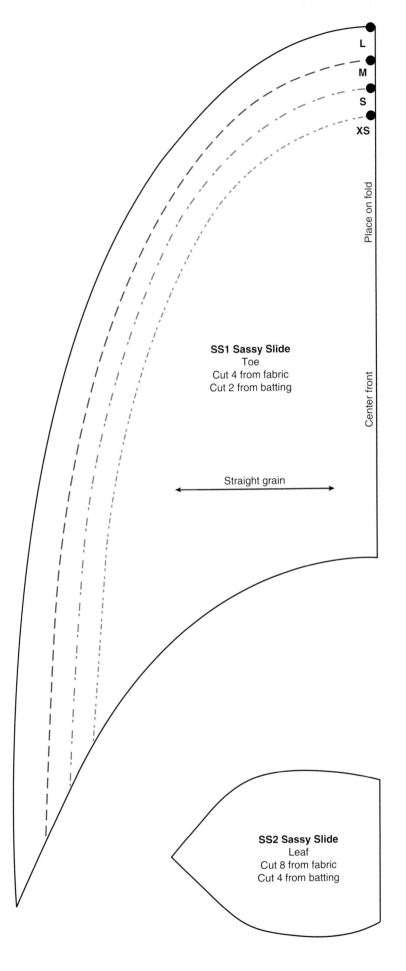

L

M

S

XS

Place on fold

Center front

SS1 Sassy Slide
Toe
Cut 4 from fabric
Cut 2 from batting

Straight grain

SS2 Sassy Slide
Leaf
Cut 8 from fabric
Cut 4 from batting

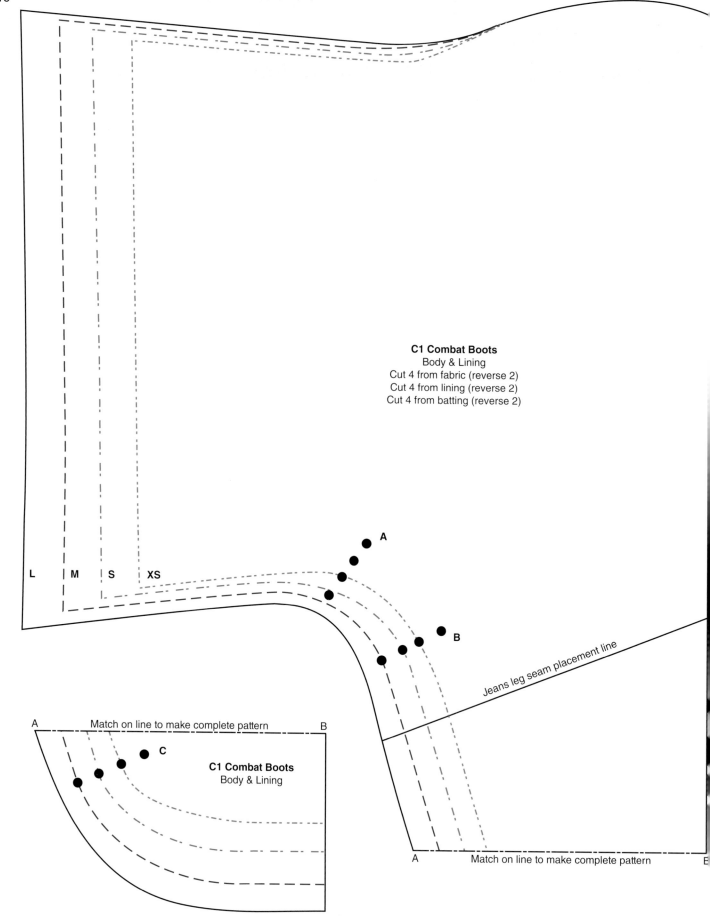

C1 Combat Boots
Body & Lining
Cut 4 from fabric (reverse 2)
Cut 4 from lining (reverse 2)
Cut 4 from batting (reverse 2)

A

L   M   S   XS

B

Jeans leg seam placement line

A   Match on line to make complete pattern   B

C

C1 Combat Boots
Body & Lining

A   Match on line to make complete pattern   B

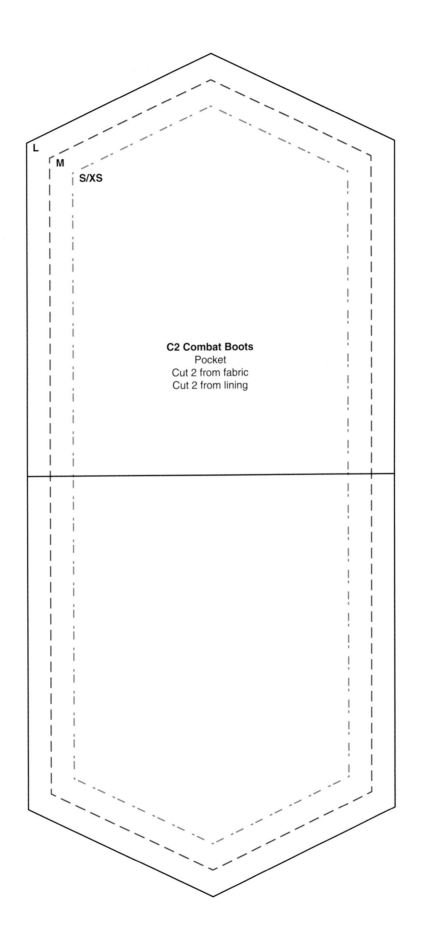

C2 Combat Boots
Pocket
Cut 2 from fabric
Cut 2 from lining

L
M
S/XS

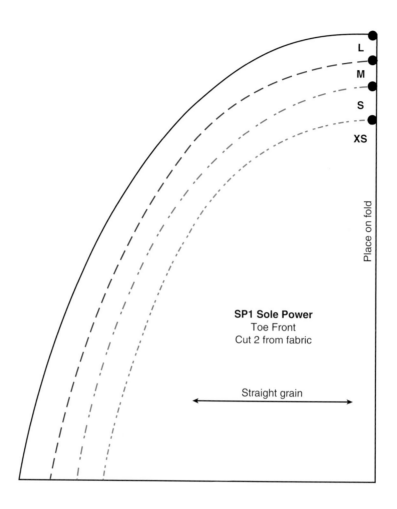

L

M

S

XS

Place on fold

SP1 Sole Power
Toe Front
Cut 2 from fabric

Straight grain

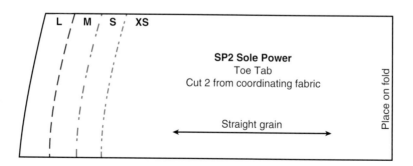

L   M   S   XS

SP2 Sole Power
Toe Tab
Cut 2 from coordinating fabric

Place on fold

Straight grain

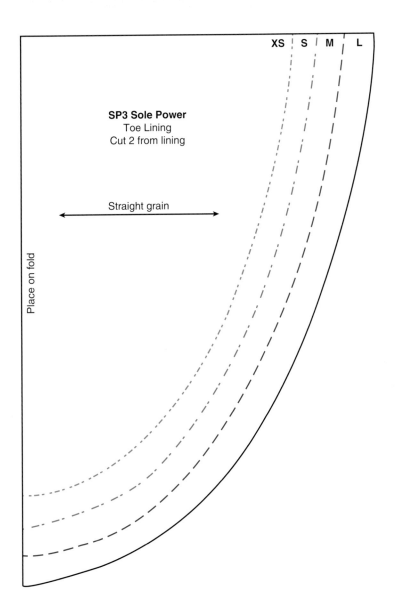

SP3 Sole Power
Toe Lining
Cut 2 from lining

Straight grain

Place on fold

XS S M L

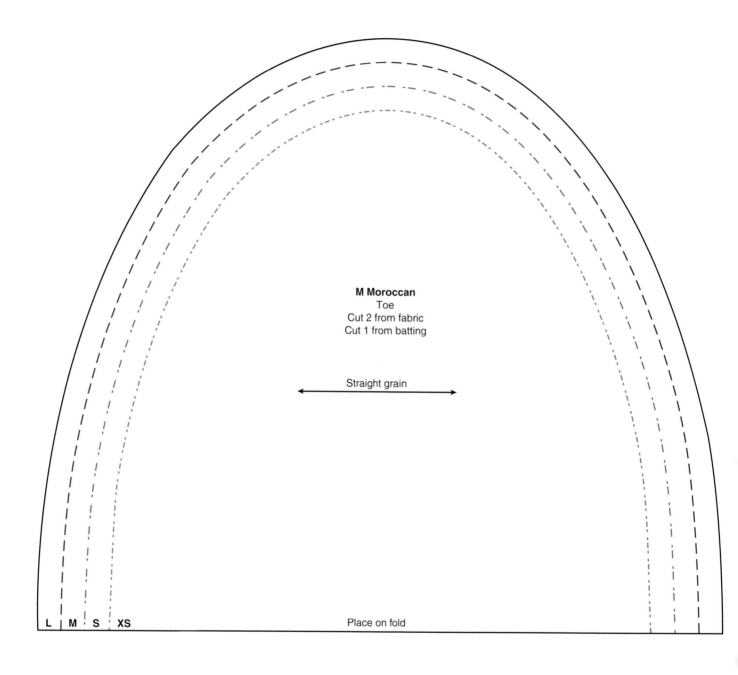

M Moroccan
Toe
Cut 2 from fabric
Cut 1 from batting

Straight grain

L M S XS

Place on fold

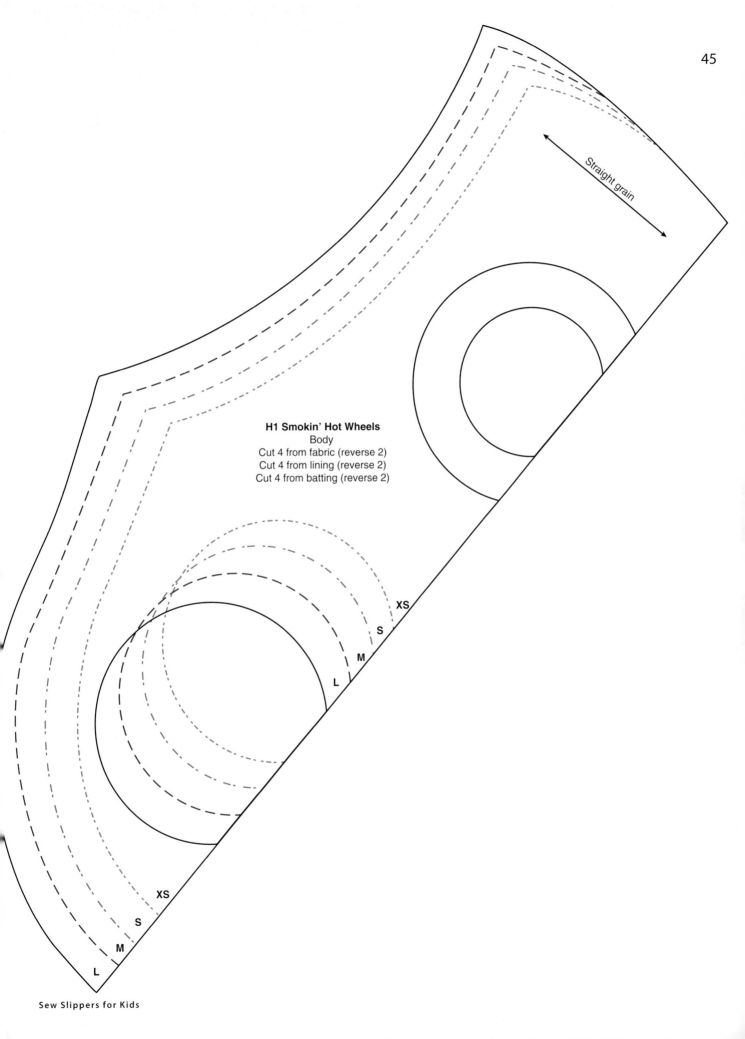

Straight grain

H1 Smokin' Hot Wheels
Body
Cut 4 from fabric (reverse 2)
Cut 4 from lining (reverse 2)
Cut 4 from batting (reverse 2)

XS
S
M
L

XS
S
M
L

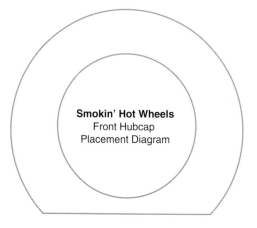

Smokin' Hot Wheels
Front Hubcap
Placement Diagram

H3 Smokin' Hot Wheels
Front Hubcap
Cut 4 per pattern instructions

H4 Smokin' Hot Wheels
Back Hubcap
Cut 4 per pattern instructions

H2 Smokin' Hot Wheels
Wheel
Cut 4 front wheels per pattern instructions
Cut 4 back wheels per pattern instructions

Back cutting line

Front cutting line

Sources

- **Clotilde**
  Slipper Gripper
  Flower Frill Template (Sole Power design)

- **Coats and Clark**
  All Thread

Photo Index

6

8

10

12

15

18

21

23

26